Love,
Paris

Published by Cider Mill Press, an imprint of HarperCollins Focus LLC,
501 Nelson Place, Nashville, TN 37214 USA.

13-Digit ISBN: 978-1-40035-585-3
10-Digit ISBN: 1-40035-585-0

Books published by Cider Mill Press Book Publishers are available at special discounts for bulk purchases in the United States by corporations, institutions, and other organizations. For more information, please contact the publisher.

cidermillpress.com

HarperCollins Publishers, Macken House, 39/40 Mayor Street Upper,
Dublin 1, D01 C9W8, Ireland (https://www.harpercollins.com)

Cover design by Shannon Johnson-Pynes
Interior design by Ben Sampson

Typography: Adobe Garamond Pro, Gotham, Nautica, Semplicita, StilsonDisplayCond

Image Credits: Photos on pages 4, 10–11, 104, 134, 200, 231 used under official license from Unsplash; pages 12, 42, 74, 166 used under official license from pexels.com; pages 22–23, 33, 41, 50, 57, 60, 85, 89, 90, 93, 94, 97, 98, 101, 102, 116, 141, 142, 145, 165, 190, 193, 197, 216, 219 used under official license from Shutterstock.com. All other photos courtesy of Cider Mill Press.

Printed in Malaysia

26 27 28 29 30 PJM 5 4 3 2 1

First Edition

Love, Paris

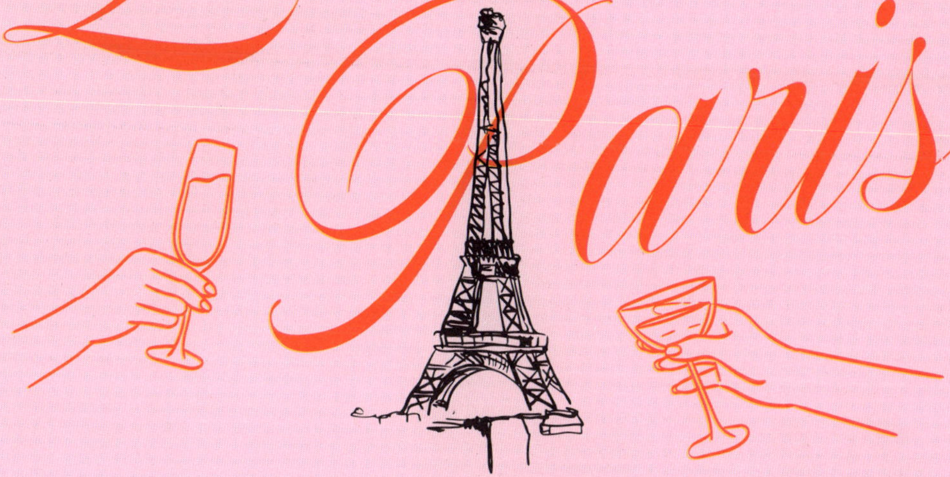

THE ART OF FRENCH COCKTAILS

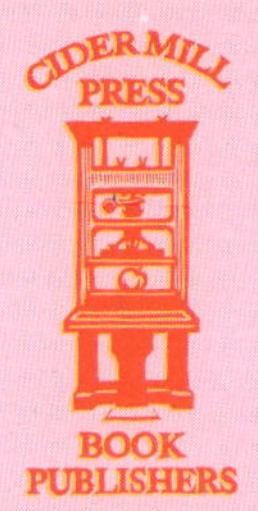

CONTENTS

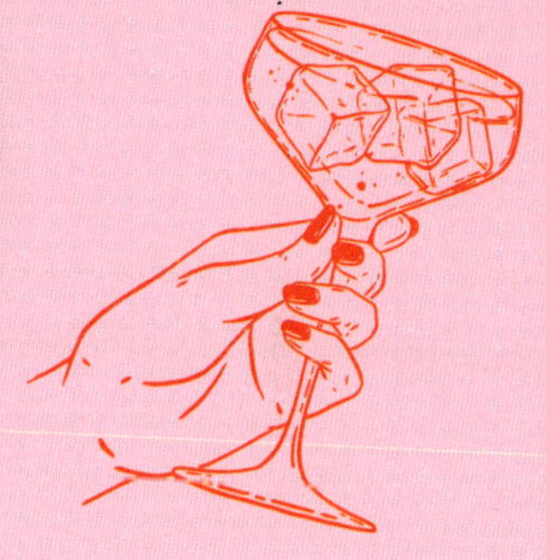

INTRODUCTION

This book is a love letter to the City of Light and the effortless charm and artistry it inspires in every moment. Every boulevard, balcony, and bistro hums with stories of passion and adventure, of stolen kisses and sparkling conversations that last until dawn.

Here, each drink is crafted in the spirit of Paris: elegant yet daring, timeless yet unpredictable. Some sparkle like the Eiffel Tower at midnight; others float like a jazz melody drifting through Montmartre in the midday sun. These cocktails capture the essence of the city—its beauty, its bite, and its ability to turn even heartbreak into art.

So raise a glass to unforgettable nights, to love that dances through the city streets, and to Paris: the city that reminds us that life, like a perfect cocktail, is meant to be savored.

FRENCH COCKTAILING RULES

- French love rules more than most cultures and as in everything else in French life, there are strict drinking guidelines to be followed.
- DO clink glasses with everyone in the group, wishing each other "Santé" (to health).
- Do NOT cross arms with others in your group—this brings bad luck.
- DO make eye contact with the person whose glass you're clinking, or risk seven years of bad sex. Horrors!
- DO bring a good bottle of Champagne to your hostess.
- DO NOT open the Champagne before your guest of honor enters.
- ALWAYS remember: Moderation is a girl's best friend.
- And the worst one: Wait until your host pours you more wine.
- P.S. We've always said rules were made to be broken.

COCKTAIL NOMENCLATURE

APÉRITIF/DIJESTIF: A drink that stimulates your appetite or a drink that helps you digest your meal. Examples of apéritifs are Suze and soda, any Champagne-based cocktail, Lillet or a kir. Dijestifs are drinks made with brandy, Chartreuse, Bénédictine, or calvados.

BITTERS: There are two different categories of bitters. There are bitter liqueurs, which are used as a modifier or base for a variety of cocktails. Examples include Campari, Suze, Aperol, Amaro, and Cocchi Rosa. There are also "bitters," which come in small bottles, the most well known being Angostura bitters. These are infused and very flavorful alcohol-based liquids typically used in extremely small quantities to add depth to a cocktail. They are made by a variety of companies and come in a myriad of flavors such as orange, chocolate, celery, and lavender, to name but a few.

A note on bitters: Bitters are a key ingredient in today's craft cocktails. Stock up on a variety of flavors. There are a number of excellent companies making bitters in the U.S. and beyond including Bitter End, Fee's, Scrappy's, Bob's, and Bittermans. Aromatic and orange are the most common flavor profiles. A sampler pack, which several of the companies offer, is a great idea.

CORDIALS: A sweetened and flavored liquor. Cordials and liqueurs are basically the same thing, except in the UK where a cordial is a sweet syrup without alcohol.

LIQUEUR: An alcoholic substance that is typically sweeter than a liquor and made by combining a distilled spirit with something sweet and flavorful such as fruit, coffee, cream, chocolate, herbs, or spices. Examples are cassis, Kahlúa, Irish cream, crème de menthe, and Grand Marnier.

VERMOUTH: Vermouth is an aromatized, fortified wine that can be white, amber, rose, or red. Historically, vermouth coming from Italy was sweet and from France was dry, but now manufacturers all over make a range of colors and versions in response to consumer appetite.

LIQUOR: An alcoholic substance made from grains, plants, or sugar cane and fermented to be drunk straight or combined and used as the base of a cocktail. Examples are rum, vodka, gin, brandy, tequila, whiskey, and cachaça (a sugar cane–based alcohol made in Brazil).

GRENADINE: A popular pomegranate juice and sugar syrup used in cocktails. It can easily be made at home, which results in a better end-product than bottled versions. However, if you don't have the time for DIY, almost all syrups are available over the counter.

BAR TOOLS

Crafting the perfect cocktail takes a mix of finesse, timing, and the right tools to make it all come together perfectly. Some drinks practically pour themselves, while others invite a little extra care and attention to truly shine. That's where a well-equipped bar comes in. Here's what every home Parisian mixologist should have at hand.

COCKTAIL SHAKER
STRAINER
JIGGER
KNIFE
BOTTLE OPENER
CORKSCREW
COCKTAIL STIRRER
MUDDLER
JUICER
ZESTER

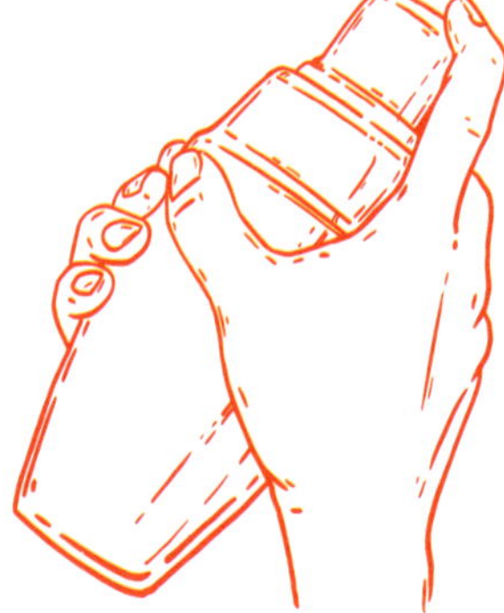

A NOTE ABOUT INGREDIENTS (AND SUBSTITUTIONS)

When a specific gin, rum, or other spirit is named, it's chosen for its unique character and flavor profile. To recreate each drink exactly as served by the professionals, use the listed ingredients and brands. That being said, substitutions are totally fair game—swapping one premium vodka for another won't make much difference. But tread carefully with vermouths, liqueurs, and bitters, where brand and balance can dramatically alter the taste. Stock up on key ingredients before attempting the more complex cocktails, and mix with confidence. And, of course, feel free to experiment with different garnishes, or even skip them entirely if you're short on time or materials.

SIMPLE SYRUP: A number of cocktails call for simple syrup. Fortunately, simple syrup is as simple to make as its name suggests. Combine water and white granulated sugar in a 1:1 ratio in a pan over medium heat, stirring until sugar is completely dissolved. Do not boil. The syrup should keep for about a month in the fridge. You can add a dash of vodka to extend the shelf life.

EACH CHAPTER CELEBRATES A DIFFERENT PARISIAN MOOD: the buzz of a crowded bistro, the serenity of a stroll along the Seine, the sparkle of a garden gala. Every drink tells a story of the city. Its rhythm and light shine through in these sippable testaments to Paris's irresistible charm. Mix them for yourself or share with friends who love a good toast and an even better view. It's time to sip, stir, and savor Paris in all her moods.

CASTEL CAFE

STREET CORNER SIPPING

This chapter brings to life the charm and magic of sitting in a corner café in the city of love. Whether you're picturing yourself enjoying an espresso and an eclair in the morning or falling in love over a romantic dinner for two in the glow of the evening, this chapter has the perfect cocktail to embody your dreams.

Cobblestone Kiss

1 OZ. TANQUERAY SEVILLA GIN

1 OZ. ORANGE WINE

½ OZ. VANILLA SYRUP

2 DASHES ORANGE BITTERS

½ OZ. PIERRE FERRAND DRY CURAÇAO

1 DROP ORANGE BLOSSOM WATER

3 OZ. PROSECCO

BLOOD ORANGE WHEEL (GARNISH)

ORANGE TWIST (GARNISH)

Fill a highball glass with ice.

In a cocktail shaker with ice, combine all the ingredients except the prosecco and shake vigorously.

Strain the drink into the highball glass.

Top with prosecco and gently stir.

Garnish with a blood orange wheel and an orange twist.

Combining the orange flavors of Tanqueray's Sevilla gin, curaçao, orange wine, orange bitters, and orange blossom—plus a blood orange and orange twist garnish—this drink refreshes like a great Spritz should.

DANTE

A French-ified version of a true American classic, the Whiskey Sour.

1½ OZ. BRENNE WHISKY (OR ANOTHER SWEET WHISKEY SUCH AS JAMESON'S)

1–2 OZ. FRESH LEMON JUICE

1½ TEASPOONS SIMPLE SYRUP (SEE PAGE 9)

1½ TEASPOONS LUXARDO MARASCHINO LIQUEUR

LUXARDO MARASCHINO OR OTHER COCKTAIL CHERRIES (GARNISH)

Fill a rocks glass with ice.

Add all the ingredients to a cocktail shaker with ice.

Shake vigorously then strain into the rocks glass.

Garnish with cocktail cherries.

Café Creation

This coffee Negroni may be inspired by an everyday drink, but it is anything but typical. For this cocktail, you use vodka instead of gin, amaretto in place of vermouth, and Cordial Caffè Lucano Anniversario in place of the Campari. The mix will have a nutty, sweet taste and a creamy texture.

1 OZ. CORDIAL CAFFÈ LUCANO ANNIVERSARIO

⅔ OZ. ADRIATICO AMARETTO

1⅓ OZ. VODKA

⅓ OZ. VANILLA SYRUP

Fill a rocks glass with ice.

Add all the ingredients to a mixing glass with ice and stir.

Strain the cocktail into the rocks glass.

1 OZ. VODKA

1 OZ. COCONUT WATER, NOT FROM CONCENTRATE (SUCH AS HARMLESS HARVEST)

1 OZ. FRESH WATERMELON JUICE (SEE PAGE 23)

CHILLED PROSECCO, TO TOP (ABOUT 2 OZ.)

LIME WEDGE AND COURSE SALT, FOR THE RIM

FRESH HERB LEAVES (GARNISH)

Jaunty Beret

Fresh watermelon and coconut water make this drink particularly hydrating, while a low-alcohol content makes it appropriate for daytime drinking in the hot sun. Though watermelon juice will take a few extra minutes to prepare in advance, the rest of the drink is simply layered in the glass—no shaking or stirring required.

Chill the vodka, coconut water, watermelon juice, and prosecco in advance in the coldest part of your refrigerator for at least 3 hours.

Partially rim a chilled rocks glass by dragging a lime wedge over half of the edge and dipping it in a small plate or bowl filled with coarse salt.

Into the prepared glass, pour the chilled vodka, coconut water, and watermelon juice over one king watermelon cube. Top carefully with the prosecco.

Garnish with a fresh herb of choice, such as fennel fronds, mint, or celery leaves.

WATERMELON JUICE

To juice a watermelon, scoop out the flesh and place it in the container of an electric blender. Cover and blend on high speed for about 5 seconds or just until liquified. Strain the mixture through a fine mesh sieve, stirring occasionally to speed up the process, and store in the refrigerator (best used within 24 hours, maximum 3 days).

1½ OZ. CAMPARI

⅘ OZ. TANQUERAY LONDON DRY GIN

⅘ OZ. QUAGLIA BERGAMOT LIQUEUR

⅓ OZ. CARPANO ANTICA FORMULA VERMOUTH

BASIL LEAF (GARNISH)

LEMON PEEL (GARNISH)

Fill an old-fashioned glass with ice.

In a mixing glass, very lightly muddle two-thirds of a basil leaf.

Add all the ingredients and ice to the mixing glass.

Stir and strain the cocktail into the old-fashioned glass.

Garnish with the remaining basil and a lemon peel.

Like a charming and unexplored side street, this drink is nothing but pleasant surprises. The bergamot liqueur adds an element of bitter citrus to the mix. The slightly muddled basil brings out a pepperiness and helps elevate this drink for a perfect start to any night.

SPICY SALT, FOR THE RIM

1 OZ. TEQUILA CURADO ESPADÍN

½ OZ. AMARETTO LIQUEUR

1 OZ. WHITE BITTER

⅘ OZ. LEMON JUICE

½ OZ. BITTER ORANGE JUICE

This cocktail combines sour, bitter, and sweet flavors in wonderful ways. The tequila used here is particularly smoky, while the spicy salt rim will bring a little heat and a savory kick after each sip.

Rim a coupette with spicy salt.

Add all the ingredients to a cocktail shaker with ice and shake vigorously for 15 seconds.

Double-strain the cocktail into the coupette.

Espresso Elegance

1½ OZ. ESPRESSO, COOLED

1 OZ. AMARO AVERNA

½ OZ. ESPOLÓN BLANCO TEQUILA

½ OZ. ORGEAT

¼ OZ. DARK CRÈME DE CACAO

3 DASHES CHOCOLATE BITTERS

COFFEE BEANS (GARNISH)

This is a standout variation from the ever-popular Espresso Martini. The twist here is replacing vodka with tequila and adding the amaro. The Espolón Blanco is so smooth, you probably won't even notice the difference.

Add all the ingredients to a cocktail shaker with ice and shake vigorously.

Strain the cocktail into a chilled coupe glass.

Garnish with coffee beans.

DANTE

HONEY SYRUP

Measure out 128 grams (or, in a pinch, ⅓ cup) very hot water and 200 grams (or, in a pinch, ⅔ cup) honey. Stir or shake rapidly in a sealed container until completely combined. Store in the fridge. Yields about 8 ounces..

1½ OZ. KROGSTAD AQUAVIT

½ OZ. FRESH, STRAINED LIME JUICE

½ OZ. HONEY SYRUP (SEE RECIPE AT LEFT)

CHILLED CHAMPAGNE, TO TOP (ABOUT 2 OZ.)

STAR ANISE POD (GARNISH)

Combine the aquavit, lime juice, and honey syrup in a cocktail shaker filled with ice. Shake hard for 15 seconds, then strain into a chilled Champagne glass.

Top with chilled Champagne, by pouring carefully and slowly down the side of the glass to reduce foam.

Garnish with a star anise pod.

A wintry take on the classic French 75, this recipe showcases aquavit: a neutral spirit distilled from grain or potato and then flavored with a wide range of spices and botanicals.

Canoodling by Candlelight

1½ OZ. FRENCH GIN (SUCH AS CITADELLE)

½ OZ. SUZE

1 OZ. DRY VERMOUTH (FRENCH-MADE NOILLY PRAT OR DOLIN)

ORANGE TWIST (GARNISH)

Add all the ingredients to a rocks glass over several large chunks of ice and stir.

Garnish with an orange twist.

VARIATION

This drink can also be shaken and strained into a chilled martini glass.

This French twist on the classic Negroni is perfect for an intimate evening date.

Terrace Toast

Margarita fans (aren't we all?): this might just be a game changer for you. All of the tart, juicy lime and sharp tequila taste of the original, enlivened by a little joyful Parisian effervescence.

LIME WEDGE AND SALT, FOR THE RIM

1½ OZ. BLANCO TEQUILA

¾ OZ. GRAND MARNIER ORANGE-FLAVORED LIQUEUR

½ OZ. FRESH, STRAINED LIME JUICE

¼ OZ. SIMPLE SYRUP (SEE PAGE 9)

PINCH OF SALT

CHILLED CHAMPAGNE, TO TOP

Wet the rim of a chilled Champagne glass with a cut lime, then dip it lightly in coarse salt to coat. Set aside.

Combine the tequila, liqueur, lime juice, syrup, and salt in a cocktail shaker filled with ice. Shake hard for 15 seconds, then strain into the prepared salted glass or a plain chilled Champagne glass.

Top with chilled Champagne by pouring carefully and slowly down the side of the glass to reduce foam.

1½ OZ. EMPRESS 1908 GIN

1 OZ. SIMPLE SYRUP (SEE PAGE 9)

1 OZ. FRESHLY SQUEEZED LEMON

JUICE

1 TEASPOON THYME TINCTURE

1½ OZ. SODA WATER

THYME SPRIG (GARNISH)

LEMON WHEEL, THINLY SLICED (GARNISH)

This cocktail has all the charm and deep feeling of a long-treasured poem. And few drinks can make you feel right at home in such mellow luxury as this fizzy botanical sipper.

Add all of the ingredients except the soda water to a cocktail shaker with ice and shake.

Strain the cocktail into a Champagne flute and top with the soda water.

Garnish with a thyme sprig and a thinly sliced lemon wheel.

Stockings & Rouge

2 OZ. CHILLED APEROL

¾ OZ. FRESH, STRAINED BLOOD ORANGE JUICE

CHILLED PROSECCO, TO TOP (ABOUT 2 OZ.)

HALVED BLOOD ORANGE SLICE AND ROSEMARY (GARNISH)

A seasonal take on the Aperol Spritz, with the decidedly brunch-appropriate addition of blood orange juice and its signature deep red hue. Low in alcohol and high on simplicity—no shaking, stirring, or syrups included—it's the very definition of enticement that will keep you coming back for more.

Pour the chilled Aperol and blood orange juice into an ice-filled glass (rocks or wine glasses both work well), then top carefully with the chilled prosecco.

Garnish with a halved orange slice and a sprig of rosemary.

½ OZ. DARK CHOCOLATE LIQUEUR (MONIN BRAND IS PREFERRED)

¾ OZ. KAHLÚA

1¼ OZ. STOLICHNAYA HOT VODKA (OR ANY SPICY VODKA)

¾ OZ. PEAT MONSTER WHISKY

If you like chocolate, you'll love this one! Here's a drink that can convert a non-whisky lover into one. Created at Harry's Bar, Paris.

Stir all the ingredients in a cocktail glass with ice.

Strain and serve in a martini glass, no garnish needed.

PLAZA-ATHENEE

EASY ELEGANCE

Paris has long been hailed as a global hot spot of sophisticated culture. From the visionary fashion and top-rate cuisine to vibrant performances and grand parties housed within gorgeous architecture, this city is the epicenter of elegance. Use the drinks in this chapter to bring Paris's signature sparkle to any moment.

Haute Couture

1½ OZ. GIN (SUCH AS PLYMOUTH)

¾ OZ. FRESH, STRAINED LEMON JUICE

¾ OZ. RHUBARB SYRUP (SEE RECIPE AT RIGHT)

CHILLED CHAMPAGNE, TO TOP (ABOUT 2 OZ.)

RHUBARB RIBBONS (GARNISH)

Tangy, tart, candy-colored rhubarb adds a vibrant seasonal touch to the classic French 75. The seasonal syrup used to make this drink can be used in place of simple syrup in just about any cocktail for a cheerful dose of bright, fragrant spring flavor.

Combine the gin, lemon juice, and rhubarb syrup in a cocktail shaker filled with ice. Shake hard for 15 seconds, then strain into a chilled Champagne glass.

Top with chilled Champagne by pouring carefully and slowly down the side of the glass to reduce foam.

Garnish with rhubarb ribbons.

RHUBARB SYRUP

Combine ¾ pound chopped rhubarb in a saucepan with 1 cup water, 1 cup cane sugar, and 1 vanilla bean, split lengthwise. Bring to a boil over medium-high heat, stirring occasionally, then lower heat and cover. Let simmer gently for 5 minutes, then remove from heat.

Stir in ¼ teaspoon orange blossom water, replace lid, and let cool to room temperature. Refrigerate overnight (or at least 8 hours), then strain through a fine mesh sieve. Reserve the strained, broken-down rhubarb for use as a compote, and store both syrup and compote in the fridge. Yields about 14 ounces.

6 STRAWBERRIES, THINLY SLICED

20 MEDIUM-TO-LARGE THAI BASIL LEAVES

1 CUP GRAND MARNIER ORANGE-FLAVORED LIQUEUR

CHILLED SPARKLING ROSÉ, TO TOP (ABOUT 3 OZ. PER DRINK)

STRAWBERRY SLICE (GARNISH)

Strawberries and Thai basil, known for its spicy anise aroma, make one of the best sweet and savory combinations. An overnight infusion requires little prep (simply slice the strawberries and submerge them in a liqueur), with loads of fresh flavor and easy day-of assembly.

Combine the strawberries, basil, and liqueur in sealed container and let sit at room temperature for 8 hours or overnight. Strain through a fine mesh sieve and let chill in the refrigerator, covered, for at least 3 hours (or 1 hour in the freezer).

For each cocktail, pour 1 ounce of the infusion into a chilled Champagne glass, then top carefully with chilled sparkling rosé.

Cut a slit in the strawberry slice and perch it on the rim of the glass.

Fashion Week

1¼ OZ. FRESH POMEGRANATE PUREE

PROSECCO, TO TOP

SPLASH VODKA

ROSE PETAL (GARNISH)

This drink is light, has hints of sweetness and tartness from the pomegranates, and the prosecco tickles your throat on the way down. Its vibrant red color gives the cocktail a seductive quality and is a great opener to start off any event.

Pour the pomegranate puree into a Champagne flute.

Fill the rest of the glass with prosecco and top it off with a splash of vodka.

Garnish with a rose petal.

Hall of Mirrors

2 OZ. BEEFEATER LONDON DRY GIN

1 OZ. DOLIN DRY VERMOUTH

½ OZ. TRIPLE SEC OR COINTREAU

3 DASHES ABSINTHE (VIEUX PONTARLIER BRAND IS PREFERRED)

LEMON TWIST (GARNISH)

This perfectly mirror-like drink brings to life the elegance of one of Versaille's most famous architectural elements. The recipe comes courtesy of Phil Ward, bartender at Death & Co., New York City.

Stir all the ingredients in a mixing glass over ice.

Strain into a coupe glass.

Garnish with a lemon twist.

Showgirl Shimmy

1½ OZ. MARTINI & ROSSI RISERVA SPECIALE BITTER VERMOUTH

1 OZ. MARTINI & ROSSI PROSECCO

1 OZ. SODA WATER

½ OZ. ST-GERMAIN ELDERFLOWER LIQUEUR

½ OZ. PINEAPPLE SHRUB

LIME WHEEL (GARNISH)

This Spritz is a really fun way to start off an evening. The vermouth is nice and bitter, the elderflower liqueur is sweet, the pineapple is tart and fruity, and the prosecco and soda water provide the bubbles.

Add all the ingredients to a Collins glass with ice and stir.

Garnish with a lime wheel.

MARTINI & ROSSI
TORINO
ITALIA
MARTINI&ROSSI
BITTER
LIQUEUR
APERITIVO
1872
MADE WITH 100%
NATURAL INGREDIENTS
750ml 28.5% alc./vol.
ESTRATTI DI
ERBE AROMATICHE
PESSIONE-TORINO
MARTINI & ROSSI PESSIONE · TORINO · ITALIA

Glittering Gala

2 OZ. MARTINI & ROSSI ROSSO SWEET VERMOUTH

3 OZ. SODA WATER

LEMON TWIST (GARNISH)

The combination of vermouth and soda is one of life's simple pleasures. Martini & Rossi makes a perfect not-too-sweet vermouth and when mixed with soda water, it brightens, refreshes, and tickles your nostrils. This drink proves that you don't need much to have a magical evening.

Fill a highball glass with ice.

Add the vermouth, top with soda water, and stir.

Garnish with a lemon twist.

1 OZ. GIN

½ OZ. CAMPARI

¾ OZ. CINZANO EXTRA DRY VERMOUTH

LEMON ZEST (GARNISH)

Fill a rocks glass with ice.

Pour all the ingredients directly into the glass and stir.

Garnish with a lemon zest.

Like a less sweet Negroni, this cocktail has all the class of an upscale Parisian lounge, with all the sass of a soulful cabaret.

Meyer lemons, pomelos, blood oranges—the perfect way to show off the nuances in each variety of citrus is by making each into a pure citrus cordial (i.e., a juice and zest syrup) sous vide, then topping them off with Champagne. Adding the peels unlocks all of the citrus's most complex floral and bitter notes, which you just can't access by using the juice alone. Don't worry if you don't have the gear—anyone can achieve similar results by letting the mixture of zest, juice, and sugar sit overnight before straining. Turn the page to see the instructions for the cordial and the drink.

FRESH, ORGANIC CITRUS (FOR EVERY CUP OF CORDIAL, YOU WILL NEED ABOUT ¾ CUP CITRUS JUICE)

SUGAR

CHILLED CHAMPAGNE, TO TOP (ABOUT 4 OZ.)

CITRUS TWIST (GARNISH)

TO MAKE THE CORDIAL

Using a peeler, remove the zest from the citrus in wide strips, avoiding the bitter white pith as much as possible. Use a paring knife to slice or scrape off any excess pith from each strip.

Juice the citrus, then weigh the juice on a kitchen scale (alternate method: measure by volume in a measuring cup). Add the juice to a blender, then weigh or measure out an equal amount of sugar and add that to the blender as well. Blend on high speed until the sugar dissolves.

If using the sous vide method, carefully transfer the peels and juice/sugar mixture to a plastic bag, then seal according to sous vide instructions. Submerge in a 135°F water bath for 2 hours, then plunge the bag into an ice bath to cool. Strain and use immediately, or store in the fridge for up to 2 weeks.

If using the overnight method, combine the peels and juice/sugar mixture in a tightly sealed container, and let sit in the fridge overnight (or at least 8 hours). Strain and use immediately, or store in the fridge for up to two weeks.

TO MAKE THE DRINK

Add ¾ ounce citrus cordial to a chilled Champagne glass, then top carefully with chilled Champagne. Garnish with a fresh citrus twist.

1½ OZ. MAROLO MILLA CAMOMILE GRAPPA LIQUEUR

1 OZ. STRAWBERRY SYRUP

½ OZ. MAROLO BAROLO CHINATO

½ OZ. LEMON JUICE

DEHYDRATED CHERRY (GARNISH)

FRESH MINT (GARNISH)

Created by mixologist Amie Ward when working at Aggio Restaurant in Baltimore, Maryland, this cocktail is very sweet and floral. Marolo's Camomile Grappa has chamomile notes while the Chinato has a bit of spice. The strawberry syrup and lemon juice add a sugary and tart finish that is incredibly satisfying.

Add all the ingredients to a shaker with ice and shake vigorously.

Double-strain into a chilled martini glass.

Garnish with a dehydrated cherry and fresh mint sprig.

1⅓ OZ. AMARO LUCANO

1 OZ. MEZCAL

⅔ OZ. VANILLA LIQUEUR

ORANGE SLICE (GARNISH)

This cocktail combines the bittersweetness of a classic Italian amaro with the smokiness of mezcal and the sweet aromatic notes of vanilla liqueur. Fans of the Old Fashioned might find this oddly familiar (mixing a spirit with a sweet and a bitter component), though the differences certainly outweigh the similarities.

Add ice to a rocks glass.

Add the Amaro Lucano, mezcal, and vanilla liqueur to a mixing glass and stir.

Strain the cocktail into the rocks glass.

Garnish with a slice of orange.

Served in a Champagne coupe, this stunning, amber-colored drink mixes the smoothness of Vecchia Romagna brandy with the well-balanced combo of sugar and bitterness. When you top it off with Champagne, the drink becomes lighter and more effervescent and can be used for any type of celebration.

1 SUGAR CUBE

2 DASHES ANGOSTURA BITTERS

1⅔ OZ. VECCHIA ROMAGNA TRE BOTTI

CHAMPAGNE, TO TOP

SPRUCE ESSENCE (GARNISH)

EDIBLE FLOWERS (GARNISH)

Place the sugar cube in a Champagne coupe. Soak the cube with the Angostura bitters.

Add the Vecchia Romagna to a mixing glass with ice and stir until it is chilled and diluted.

Strain the drink into the coupe with the sugar cube.

Top off with Champagne.

Garnish with spruce essence and edible flowers.

Smoking Suit

1 OZ. BLENDED SCOTCH

½ OZ. CINNAMON SYRUP (SEE RECIPE AT RIGHT)

½ OZ. PINEAPPLE JUICE

¼ OZ. FRESH, STRAINED LIME JUICE

1 DASH ANGOSTURA BITTERS

CHILLED CHAMPAGNE (ABOUT 1 OZ.), TO TOP

CHARRED PINEAPPLE WEDGE

Smoky peat notes from the scotch and a kick of cinnamon spice say "autumn," while the pineapple and lime take a distinctly tropical bent. It is essentially a spiced, sparkling whiskey sour, but a lot more fun.

Before you mix the cocktail, char a pineapple wedge on a grill or under a broiler set to medium high, just until lightly blackened. Use a cocktail pick to balance the charred wedge on the rim of a chilled glass.

Combine the scotch, cinnamon syrup, pineapple juice, lime juice, and bitters in a cocktail shaker filled with ice. Shake hard for 15 seconds, then strain into a chilled Champagne glass.

Top carefully with the chilled Champagne.

CINNAMON SYRUP

Break up 3 standard cinnamon sticks (about 3 inches long) in the bottom of a sturdy saucepan until they are smallish shards (a wooden mallet or muddler works well for this). Add 1 cup of water and 1 cup of sugar. Bring to a boil, stirring occasionally, then lower heat and simmer, covered, for 5 minutes. Remove from heat and let stand, still covered, at room temperature overnight. Strain through a fine mesh sieve and use immediately or store in the fridge. Yields about 2 cups.

Perfumed Panache

CHILLED PROSECCO (ABOUT 2 OZ.)

CHILLED IPA BEER (ABOUT 2 OZ.)

2 OZ. CHILLED PINEAPPLE JUICE

PINEAPPLE LEAVES OR SLICES (GARNISH)

MARASCHINO CHERRIES (GARNISH)

EDIBLE FLOWERS (GARNISH)

Beer, pineapple, and prosecco may seem like a strange combination, but try this easy summer shandy–spritz hybrid once and you'll instantly understand—it's pretty much liquid sunshine.

In a chilled highball glass or tumbler, gently pour the chilled prosecco, the chilled IPA, and the chilled pineapple juice, in that order.

Gently slide in ice cubes and arrange pineapple leaves or slices, maraschino cherries, and edible flowers on top.

Lady in Lace

1¼ OZ. YOGURT RHUM (SEE RECIPE AT RIGHT)

¾ OZ. DOLIN BLANC VERMOUTH

½ OZ. LIME-ACID CORDIAL (SEE RECIPE AT RIGHT)

This drink is a blend of funky rum and yogurt flavors. It includes a lime-acid cordial that saves you from having to shake a drink (while bringing the ticket time down to about 45 seconds), and ultimately creates the creamiest clarified Daiquiri.

In a mixing glass, stir all the ingredients over ice.

Strain into a rocks glass over a large ice cube.

Garnish with a waxflower sprig.

YOGURT RHUM

Using a whisk, thoroughly mix together 750 ml Clèment Rhum Blanc and 262 grams plain yogurt. Add 94 grams lemon juice and whisk again. Leave the mixture out at room temperature for 30 minutes. Strain through a chinois and coffee filter until clear.

LIME-ACID CORDIAL

Mix 500 grams sugar, 500 grams water, 16 grams citric acid, and 10 grams malic acid together and bring to a simmer, or use hot water to dissolve the ingredients.

CLASSIC, CLASSY & CHIC

France is the birthplace of a number of iconic cocktails. Harry's New York Bar in Paris alone is responsible for several of the most classic drinks ever created. Find the concoctions that made Paris a must-visit cocktail destination in this chapter.

Champagne Cocktail

1 DEMERARA SUGAR CUBE

ANGOSTURA BITTERS

CHILLED CHAMPAGNE, TO TOP (ABOUT 5 OZ.)

LEMON TWIST (GARNISH)

This classic cocktail is as simple as its name—just soak a sugar cube in bitters, top with bubbly, and watch it fizz. In fact, "watching it fizz" is kind of the point here. Between the ease of the recipe and the spectacle it creates, the Champagne Cocktail is a perfect party drink.

Place the demerara sugar cube on a small plate or bowl, then dash with the Angostura bitters until soaked.

Transfer the soaked sugar cube to the bottom of a chilled Champagne flute, then top slowly with the chilled Champagne by pouring carefully and slowly down the side of the glass to reduce foam.

Garnish with a lemon twist.

1½ OZ. GIN (SUCH AS PLYMOUTH)

¾ OZ. FRESH, STRAINED LEMON JUICE

½ OZ. SIMPLE SYRUP (SEE PAGE 9)

CHILLED CHAMPAGNE, TO TOP (ABOUT 2 OZ.)

LEMON TWIST (GARNISH)

This cocktail dates back to 1915 and its original name "Soixante-Quinze" referred to the French 75-millimeter field gun heavily in use during WWI. If you love the tart pop of fresh lemons, you may fall hard for this pale gold paragon. It's refreshing but elegant, vivacious but refined—the kind of cocktail that suits almost any occasion.

Combine the gin, lemon juice, and simple syrup in a cocktail shaker filled with ice. Shake hard for 15 seconds, then strain into a chilled Champagne glass.

Top with chilled Champagne by pouring carefully and slowly down the side of the glass to reduce foam.

Garnish with a lemon twist.

½ OZ. CHILLED BLACK CURRANT LIQUEUR (SUCH AS CLEAR CREEK DISTILLERY CASSIS LIQUEUR)

CHILLED CHAMPAGNE, TO TOP (ABOUT 5 OZ.)

SKEWERED MARASCHINO CHERRY (SUCH AS LUXARDO) OR BLACKBERRIES (GARNISH)

A classic cocktail that couldn't be simpler—pour chilled black currant liqueur and Champagne into a glass and call it a day. In addition to an appealingly deep plummy hue, the liqueur brings rich, tart berry notes to the table, which is perhaps why you see this cocktail return year after year for holiday toasts. Little effort, bold color, bright flavor. What's not to love?

Pour the chilled liqueur into the bottom of a Champagne glass.

Top with chilled Champagne by pouring carefully and slowly down the side of the glass to reduce foam.

Garnish with a skewered maraschino cherry or blackberries.

Champagne Sidecar

1 OZ. BRANDY (SUCH AS PIERRE FERRAND AMBRE COGNAC)

1 OZ. GRAND MARNIER ORANGE-FLAVORED LIQUEUR

½ OZ. FRESH, STRAINED LEMON JUICE

CHILLED CHAMPAGNE, TO TOP (ABOUT 1 OZ.)

ORANGE TWIST OR LEMON WHEEL (GARNISH)

THYME SPRIG

An effervescent take on a classic, the Champagne Sidecar transforms the standard brandy sour into something at once more festive and refreshing. You'll notice deeper fall fruit notes from the Cognac (like apple and pear), and a more complex tartness that comes from merging the orange liqueur and lemon juice with Champagne's tartaric and lactic acid. In other words, it opens the Sidecar up a bit to let each component sing.

Combine the brandy, liqueur, and lemon juice in a cocktail shaker filled with ice. Shake hard for 15 seconds, then strain into a chilled Champagne glass.

Top with chilled Champagne.

Garnish with an orange twist or lemon wheel and a thyme sprig.

Mimosa

2 OZ. FRESH, STRAINED ORANGE JUICE

½ OZ. GRAND MARNIER ORANGE-FLAVORED LIQUEUR

CHILLED CHAMPAGNE, TO TOP (ABOUT 3 OZ.)

3 DROPS ORANGE BLOSSOM WATER (GARNISH)

This classic French cocktail is found everywhere across the world. It is perfect for both sweet and savory meals, so while it's usually enjoyed at brunch, there is no bad time for a Mimosa.

Combine the orange juice and liqueur in a chilled Champagne glass, then top carefully with chilled Champagne.

Top with 3 drops of orange blossom water.

Boulevardier

1 OZ. SELECT APERITIVO

1 OZ. SWEET VERMOUTH

1 OZ. BOURBON

ORANGE PEEL (GARNISH)

Place a large ice cube in a rocks glass.

Combine all the ingredients in a mixing glass. Add ice and stir for 30 seconds.

Strain into the rocks glass over the ice.

Garnish with an orange peel.

The drink is easy to remember, as it has equal parts vermouth, bourbon, and aperitivo. Similar to the Negroni (replacing gin with bourbon) the Select iteration of the cocktail adds a little more complexity to the drink, as its aperitivo is more bitter and has hints of vanilla.

Between the Sheets

1 OZ. COGNAC

1 OZ. WHITE RUM

1 OZ. TRIPLE SEC

1 TBSP LEMON JUICE, FRESHLY SQUEEZED

ORANGE PEEL (GARNISH)

This drink has a somewhat sordid history, according to legend; some say it was first drunk by "ladies of the night" as an aperitif in French brothels. Later, the cocktail gained a much more upstanding reputation as a signature drink at Harry's New York Bar in Paris.

Combine all the ingredients in a cocktail shaker filled with ice and shake until chilled.

Strain into a stemmed cocktail glass.

Garnish with an orange peel.

Death in the Afternoon

¼ TO ½ OZ. ABSINTHE (TO TASTE)

CHAMPAGNE

DASH OF SIMPLE SYRUP (SEE PAGE 9)

This drink was created by Ernest Hemingway, the legendary author who knew a lot about both Paris and alcohol. Modern day adaptations tone down the absinthe from Papa's original version and make for a celebration-worthy Champagne-based cocktail.

Pour the absinthe into a chilled flute or coupe and top with Champagne

Add a dash or two of simple syrup for a slightly sweeter version.

1789

½ OZ. BONAL QUINA (OR YOUR PREFERRED APÉRITIF WHITE WINE)

½ OZ. LILLET

1⅓ OZ. BASTILLE WHISKY

In a mixing glass, add all three ingredients with ice cubes and stir.

Strain and serve in a chilled martini glass.

1789 was the year of the storming of the Bastille, the first French revolution (there were a few, in fact). Created by Harry's Bar, Paris.

Bloody Mary

SALT, CAYENNE PEPPER, AND BLACK PEPPER TO TASTE

6 DASHES WORCESTERSHIRE SAUCE

JUICE OF ½ A LEMON

2 OZ. VODKA

2 OZ. TOMATO JUICE

1 CHERRY TOMATO (GARNISH)

In a mixing glass filled with ice, combine 4 dashes of salt, 2 dashes of cayenne, and 2 dashes of black pepper.

Add the Worcestershire, lemon juice, vodka, and tomato juice.

Stir then strain into a martini glass.

Garnish with a cherry tomato.

Created by Harry's New York Bar in 1921 by bartender Ferdinand "Pete" Petiot to help a regular's hangover, what's noticeable here is what isn't included in later recipes. There's no lime (just lemon), no celery salt, no Tabasco sauce, and no horseradish.

Monaco

½ OZ. GRENADINE SYRUP

2 OZ. LEMON-LIME SODA

5 OZ. LAGER (LIGHT) BEER

This low-ABV sipper is the most popular French beer cocktail there is. Refreshing, sweet, and sure to satisfy.

Pour the grenadine syrup and lemon-lime soda into a chilled beer glass.

Hold the glass at an angle and pour the beer in against the side of the glass to avoid excess foam.

Blue Lagoon

1 OZ. VODKA

1 OZ. BLUE CURAÇAO

4 OZ. LEMONADE

SPLASH OF LIME JUICE

LEMON SLICE (GARNISH)

MARASCHINO CHERRY (GARNISH)

Place the vodka and blue curaçao in a cocktail shaker filled with ice and shake vigorously.

Fill a glass with ice and strain the mixture into it.

Top with the lemonade and lime juice.

Garnish with a slice of lemon and a maraschino cherry.

Legend has it that this recipe was created by Andrew MacElhone, the son of famed bartender Harry MacElhone. Harry made Harry's New York Bar into an iconic Paris landmark, then Andrew took over after his death and ran it for the rest of his life.

Embuscade

While no one is completely certain where this drink came from, most agree that it originated in Normandy. It's a perfect French cocktail for when you want something sweet and fruity—a little taste of the beach even when sipping on cobblestone streets.

3 OZ. COLD LAGER BEER

1 OZ. WHITE WINE (CHARDONNAY)

½ OZ. CALVADOS (APPLE BRANDY)

¼ OZ. BLACKCURRANT SYRUP

¼ OZ. LEMON JUICE

Add all the ingredients to a pint or cocktail glass.

Stir gently to combine and serve.

Colin Peter Field, chef du bar at the Ritz, says this is his favorite drink.

1 OZ. CALVADOS (OR YOUR APPLE BRANDY OF CHOICE)

A SPRIG OF MINT

1 OZ. APPLE JUICE

CHAMPAGNE, TO TOP

Put the calvados in a tumbler with the mint and muddle together, slightly bruising the mint.

Add plenty of ice and then the apple juice.

Top with Champagne.

GARDEN GALA

This chapter opens the gate to a world where blossoms, breeze, and laughter mingle in effortless harmony. These drinks make it easy to imagine picnicking in front of the Eiffel Tower or promenading through the Tuileries Garden or Luxembourg Garden. Here you'll find cocktails crafted to bottle the enchantment of the botanical life and intimate gatherings of Paris.

Balconies in Bloom

1 OZ. GRAND MARNIER ORANGE-FLAVORED LIQUEUR, CHILLED

3 DROPS ORANGE BLOSSOM WATER

CHILLED CHAMPAGNE, TO TOP (ABOUT 4 OZ.)

EDIBLE FLOWER (GARNISH)

This is one of those cocktails so simple in execution but complex in flavor that it belongs on everyone's short list. Have it up your sleeve for those nights when big impact but small effort is called for—last-minute guests, holiday parties, or even a low-key weeknight. When you can't manage much, you can still manage this cocktail. Bright, bold citrus and elegant floral notes suit every occasion.

Pour the chilled Grand Marnier and orange blossom water into a chilled champagne glass.

Top with chilled Champagne.

Garnish with an edible flower.

Baguette & Brie

Like the iconic pairing of baguette and brie cheese, these ingredients complement each other perfectly. You might ask, “Do I really need two types of bubbles for this cocktail?” Well, part of the point of the seltzer is to dilute the sweetness of the liqueur, but it also brings an extra level of fizziness that prosecco alone can’t provide.

1 OZ. FIORENTE ELDERFLOWER LIQUEUR

3 OZ. PROSECCO

2 OZ. SELTZER

SPRIG OF MINT (GARNISH)

Fill a wine glass with ice, add all the ingredients, and lightly stir.

Garnish with a large sprig of mint, gently compressing the leaves to release the oil.

Gingham Picnic

A little bit of extra effort—slicing strawberries, letting them sit in a liqueur overnight—gains you a ton of fresh, juicy payoff in what has become an instant classic seasonal spritz. This recipe yield four servings.

Combine the strawberries, tarragon, and liqueur in a sealed container and let sit at room temperature overnight, or 8 to 10 hours. Strain and store in the refrigerator (do not use until well chilled), reserving the infused strawberries for garnish.

For each cocktail, pour 2 oz. of the infused liqueur into a chilled wine glass, then carefully top with the chilled prosecco. Gently slide in ice and sliced strawberries (reserved from the infusion, or fresh).

Add a splash of balsamic vinegar and fresh sliced strawberries on top.

6 STRAWBERRIES, SLICED THIN

6 SPRIGS TARRAGON
(ABOUT 4 INCHES LONG EACH)

1 CUP LIQUEUR OF CHOICE
(SUCH AS APEROL, CAMPARI,
LILLET, OR ELDERFLOWER)

CHILLED PROSECCO, TO TOP
(ABOUT 3 OZ. PER COCKTAIL)

SPLASH OF GOOD-QUALITY
BALSAMIC VINEGAR (GARNISH)

FRESH SLICED STRAWBERRIES
(GARNISH)

Petals Pavement

¾ OZ. HIBISCUS SYRUP

½ OZ. FRESH, STRAINED LEMON JUICE

CHILLED CHAMPAGNE, TO TOP (ABOUT 5 OZ.)

LEMON WHEEL OR A FEW DROPS OF ROSEWATER (GARNISH)

Vibrant in color and tart in flavor, hibiscus tastes more like a cranberry than a flower. This recipe uses a homemade syrup, but it's so easy to make it doesn't feel particularly burdensome. Simply brew your hibiscus tea as usual, add sugar and stir.

Pour the syrup and lemon juice into a chilled Champagne glass, then top carefully with chilled Champagne.

Garnish with a lemon wheel or a few drops of rosewater.

1 OZ. FRESH, STRAINED GRAPEFRUIT JUICE

1 OZ. GRAND MARNIER ORANGE-FLAVORED LIQUEUR

3 DROPS ROSEWATER

CHILLED CHAMPAGNE, TO TOP (ABOUT 2 OZ.)

ROSE PETAL (GARNISH)

GRAPEFRUIT PEEL (GARNISH)

This floral, citrusy drink has all the charm and passion of Monet's most famous works.

Combine the grapefruit juice, liqueur, and rosewater in a cocktail shaker filled with ice. Shake hard for 15 seconds, then strain into a chilled Champagne glass.

Top with chilled Champagne by pouring carefully and slowly down the side of the glass to reduce foam.

Garnish with a rose petal and grapefruit peel.

La Vie Bohème

1½ OZ. AMONTILLADO SHERRY

1 TABLESPOON DRY CURAÇAO, PREFERABLY PIERRE FERRAND (OR YOUR FAVORITE ORANGE-FLAVORED LIQUEUR)

2 TEASPOONS SIMPLE SYRUP (SEE PAGE 9)

1 OZ. TAMARIND WATER

CHILLED DRY CHAMPAGNE, TO TOP

ORANGE SLICE (GARNISH)

SPRIG OF ROSEMARY (GARNISH)

Created by Jen Riley at the Red House, this unique Champagne cocktail has French and Portuguese elements plus a hint of the tropics.

Build this cocktail straight into a highball style glass over ice, stir, and top off with Champagne.

Garnish with an orange slice and a sprig of rosemary.

Fleur-de-lis

5 TO 6 OZ. BRUT SPARKLING WINE

⅔ OZ. AMARO LUCANO

⅔ OZ. VODKA, COLORED BLUE WITH SPIRULINA

ORANGE ESSENCE (GARNISH)

This is a tricolor drink meant to mirror the French flag (blue, white, red) and combines the bittersweetness of Amaro Lucano with the effervescence of sparkling wine, along with a hint of seaweed from the spirulina-laced vodka. Visually stunning and fun to drink, this cocktail will be a hit at any party—especially for Francophiles.

Pour the sparkling wine into a highball glass.

Add the amaro and allow it to collect at the bottom.

Top off the drink with the vodka, one spoon at a time to preserve the color layers.

Spray the glass with orange essence.

Secret Garden

This punch is tailor-made for elegant garden parties. It yields 16 servings, and its highly aromatic blooms paired with the layering of coloring and flavor makes it irresistible. If you find edible flowers too cost-prohibitive or difficult to procure, sub in 1 teaspoon rosewater or orange blossom water, and garnish with halved grapefruit slices instead.

Pour the chilled gin, chilled elderflower liqueur, lemon juice, grapefruit juice, simple syrup, and bitters into a punch bowl over 1 large block of ice. Stir rapidly until chilled, about 20 seconds.

Top carefully with the chilled Champagne, then garnish with a variety of edible flowers. Ladle a few flowers into each punch cup as you serve.

3 CUPS GIN, CHILLED

1 CUP ELDERFLOWER LIQUEUR, CHILLED

1½ CUPS FRESH, STRAINED LEMON JUICE (FROM ABOUT 6 TO 8 LEMONS)

1½ CUPS FRESH, STRAINED GRAPEFRUIT JUICE (FROM ABOUT 2 RUBY RED GRAPEFRUITS)

1½ CUPS SIMPLE SYRUP (SEE PAGE 9)

1 TEASPOON PEYCHAUD'S AROMATIC BITTERS

1 BOTTLE CHAMPAGNE, CHILLED

ABOUT ½ TO 1 CUP FLOWERS SUCH AS LAVENDER, ROSE, VIOLA, BORAGE, BEGONIA, CALENDULA, DAHLIA, DIANTHUS, HIBISCUS, NASTURTIUM, OR SNAPDRAGON, GROWN ORGANICALLY FOR CULINARY USE

¾ OZ. DEL MAGUEY VIDA MEZCAL

½ OZ. ELEPHANT SLOE GIN

⅓ OZ. VERJUS

2¾ OZ. AGUA DE JAMAICA (SEE RECIPE BELOW)

Fill a wine glass with ice.

Pour all the ingredients over and stir.

AGUA DE JAMAICA

Combine 48 g hibiscus and 42 g flower honey in 500 ml water and mix well.

Valentin, the ingenious bartender at Apicius, has found a way to marry East (Yuzu Saki), West (New York Corn Whiskey), and Middle (Antique Sherry from Spain) in one delicious, life-affirming drink!

Picturesque Pastels

1 SCOOP SORBET OF CHOICE

3 DROPS ORANGE BLOSSOM WATER AND 1 BLACKBERRY OR OTHER FRESH FRUIT (GARNISH)

CHILLED CHAMPAGNE, TO TOP (ABOUT 3 OZ.)

Equally at home during the summer and winter holidays, this dish defies seasonality. Champagne and fruit are just meant to be together, and a frozen puree in the form of a sorbet is the easiest way to access fresh fruit year-round.

Place the scoop of sorbet in a chilled dessert bowl and add 3 drops of orange blossom water.

Top with the chilled Champagne, pouring directly over the scoop.

Garnish with fresh fruit.

1 OZ. TEQUILA

½ OZ. LILLET

½ OZ. COINTREAU (OR YOUR PREFERRED TRIPLE SEC)

ORANGE JUICE

PASSION FRUIT JUICE

FRESH LIME JUICE

LIME WEDGE (GARNISH)

LEMON PEEL (GARNISH)

Summer Soirée

This is the French version of a Tequila Sunrise—tequila smoothed with Lillet, brightened by Cointreau, and lifted by a sunrise of orange, passion fruit, and fresh lime.

Put the tequila, Lillet, and Cointreau in a cocktail shaker, then add 1 part orange juice and 1 part passion fruit juice (equaling no more than as much as the liquor in the glass for a strong drink and ⅔ to ⅓ liquor for a weaker drink).

Add a healthy squeeze of lime. Shake it up well, strain and serve in a highball glass on the rocks.

Garnish with a lime wedge and lemon peel.

Lavender Reverie

1 SPRIG LAVENDER

1 GRAPEFRUIT TWIST

1½ OZ. CHILLED ELDERFLOWER LIQUEUR

CHILLED PROSECCO, TO TOP (ABOUT 3 OZ.)

The bright, almost lychee-like flavor of the elderflower shines in this simple spritz, perfect for a spring afternoon. Layer in complexity with a grapefruit twist and sprig of lavender—both are highly aromatic and lovely in the glass.

Rub the sprig of lavender and the grapefruit twist around the inside of a chilled wine glass, then set them aside.

Pour the chilled liqueur into the glass, then top carefully with the chilled prosecco. Gently slide in ice and place the lavender and grapefruit twist on top.

Promenade

½ OZ. GIN

½ OZ. GREEN CHARTREUSE

½ OZ. MARASCHINO LIQUEUR (SUCH AS LUXARDO)

½ OZ. FRESH, STRAINED LIME JUICE

CHILLED CHAMPAGNE, TO TOP

HERB SPRIG OR MARASCHINO CHERRY (GARNISH)

Combine the gin, Chartreuse, liqueur, and lime juice in a cocktail shaker filled with ice. Shake hard for 15 seconds, then strain into a chilled Champagne glass.

Top with chilled Champagne by pouring carefully and slowly down the side of the glass to reduce foam.

Garnish with an herb sprig (such as rosemary) or a skewered maraschino cherry.

This recipe is a sparkling version of the vintage Last Word cocktail. It's every bit as sharp, tart, and herbaceous as the original, but with more refreshing acidity and peppy effervescence. The addition of sparkling wine opens up each flavor and gives it room to breathe.

Sunday in the Park

This drink was created by Dale DeGroff, the modern cocktail legend. At first glance this cocktail seems similar to the Champagne Sidecar (see page 83), but on the palette you'll notice the addition of maraschino liqueur's fruity, nutty, indescribable funk.

Fill a chilled mixing glass or metal shaking tin with ice, then pour the Cognac, liqueurs, and lemon juice into the vessel. Stir rapidly with a metal bar spoon for 15 seconds, then strain into a chilled Champagne glass.

Top carefully with chilled Champagne.

Garnish with an orange twist.

¾ OZ. COGNAC (SUCH AS PIERRE FERRAND AMBRE)

½ OZ. ORANGE-FLAVORED LIQUEUR

¼ OZ. MARASCHINO LIQUEUR (SUCH AS LUXARDO)

¼ OZ. FRESH, STRAINED LEMON JUICE

CHILLED CHAMPAGNE, TO TOP (ABOUT 2 OZ.)

ORANGE TWIST (GARNISH)

STROLLING ALONG THE SEINE

These drinks capture the easy charm of a dreamy stroll along the Seine. Picture pausing by the water as boats glide past, the city moving at a calm, steady pace around you. These cocktails deliver that unmistakable Parisian ease—simple and perfect for unwinding, with just a touch of magic.

1 OZ. MARTIN MILLER'S ORIGINAL GIN

⅓ OZ. CAMPARI

⅔ OZ. LILLET BLANC

¼ OZ. TIO PEPE SHERRY

STRAWBERRIES (GARNISH)

This offshoot of a Negroni brings together Lillet Blanc and Tio Pepe Sherry to give this drink a nutty and savory flavor. The fresh strawberries are a nice touch to offset any bitterness and the large ice chunk will help keep dilution to a minimum. Just like the iconic symbol of a lasting love, this drink is an instant classic that will stand the test of time.

Add a large ice chunk to a chilled Nick & Nora glass.

Add all the ingredients to a mixing glass with ice and stir until well chilled.

Strain the cocktail into the glass.

Garnish with fresh strawberries.

GiLLi

Street Artist

⅔ OZ. ALPHA CENTAURI ESPADIN MEZCAL

⅔ OZ. CAMPARI

⅔ OZ. ANTICA TORINO VERMOUTH

⅓ OZ. VARNELLI CAFFÈ MOKA LIQUEUR

3 DASHES ANGOSTURA BITTERS

ROASTED MARSHMALLOW (GARNISH)

LEMON TWIST (GARNISH)

BLUEBERRY (GARNISH)

This version of a Negroni uses mezcal in place of gin for a smokier profile, and it also gets more bitter with some coffee liqueur—it's a really nice and unexpected touch.

Fill an old-fashioned glass with ice.

Add all the ingredients and stir.

Garnish with a roasted marshmallow, a lemon twist, and a blueberry.

Midnight Sparkle

1¼ OZ. MEZCAL

1⅔ OZ. PEAR JUICE

⅓ OZ. SIMPLE SYRUP (SEE PAGE 9)

CHAMPAGNE, TO TOP

PEAR SLICE (GARNISH)

A tribute to the sparkling lights of the Eiffel Tower at night, this bubbly drink is as festive as it is tasty.

Fill a shaker with ice, the mezcal, pear juice, and simple syrup.

Shake 4 or 5 times to aerate the cocktail.

Pour it into a Champagne flute and top with Champagne.

Garnish with the pear slice.

Moody Mime

This is a beautiful take on the classic martini via Colin Peter Field from Bar Hemingway at the Ritz.

NOILLY PRATT VERMOUTH ICE CUBE (SEE RECIPE BELOW)

GIN OR VODKA

SKEWERED OLIVES (GARNISH)

Pour your favorite gin or vodka into a frozen martini glass and add the vermouth ice cube.

VERMOUTH ICE CUBES

Add 2 parts water to 1 part vermouth and freeze in ice cube trays. The optimal proportion of vermouth to water will vary slightly depending on the vermouth and the temperature of your freezer, so don't hesitate to increase the water if cubes are not as solid as desired.

Whispered Rendezvous

3 OZ. DRY WHITE WINE

1 OZ. PEACH NECTAR

2 OZ. SELECT APERITIVO

1 OZ. SODA WATER

THYME SPRIG (GARNISH)

Pour the wine, peach nectar, and Select into a cocktail shaker with ice and shake.

Strain the mixture into a glass filled with ice.

Top with soda water and gently stir.

Garnish with a thyme sprig.

This cocktail is not only refreshing, but sweet and sparkling without being overbearing, just like a thrilling meeting with a new love. It's a wonderful summer drink.

GINGER HONEY SYRUP

Combine ¾ cup honey, ¾ cup water, and 1 large knot of ginger (about 6 inches long or 50 grams by weight, peeled and thinly sliced) in a saucepan over medium-high heat.

Bring to a boil, stirring occasionally, then reduce heat to low and let simmer 5 minutes. Remove from heat, cover, and let cool to room temperature. Refrigerate overnight (or at least 8 hours), then strain through a fine mesh sieve, discarding solids. Use immediately or store in the fridge. Yields about 10 ounces.

Sweet Serenade

1 OZ. VODKA

¾ OZ. GINGER HONEY SYRUP (SEE RECIPE AT LEFT)

½ OZ. FRESH, STRAINED LIME JUICE

CHILLED CHAMPAGNE, TO TOP (ABOUT 3 OZ.)

CANDIED GINGER OR HONEY-COMB (GARNISH)

Combine the vodka, ginger honey syrup, and lime juice in a cocktail shaker filled with ice. Shake hard for 15 seconds, then strain into a copper mug or tumbler filled with ice.

Top carefully with the chilled Champagne.

Garnish with candied ginger or honeycomb.

Like a Moscow Mule, but much, much better. Champagne is a major upgrade on standard soda when paired with a homemade, lightly spicy ginger honey syrup. Dangerously smooth and impossibly refreshing, it's a true party starter and crowd-pleaser.

Flirting by the Fountain

¾ OZ. COCCHI BAROLO CHINATO

¾ OZ. BAROLO DOCG

¾ OZ. MANDARIN JUICE

¾ OZ. AGED RHUM

MANDARIN PEEL (GARNISH)

This drink is supposed to be served warm, though you can certainly make it on ice in a low tumbler. When you warm this cocktail, the ingredients will meld together, and the result will be citrusy, sweet, and slightly earthy.

Combine all the ingredients in a low pot and heat on a stovetop over medium-low heat.

Strain the cocktail into a Rialto coupe.

Garnish with a mandarin peel.

Misty Morning

¼ CUP OF HOT CHAI TEA

½ TABLESPOON HONEY

2 OZ. BRENNE WHISKY (AN INCREDIBLY SMOOTH FRENCH-PRODUCED WHISKY)

CINNAMON STICK (GARNISH)

SLICE OF LEMON (GARNISH)

Similar to the age-old hot toddy, your grandma's cure for a cold, this French version uses a very smooth French whisky aged in Cognac barrels. But then we add Indian spiced chai tea. You won't need a cold to drink this yummy concoction; any misty day will create the right setting.

In a mug with the hot tea, add the honey and whisky.

Serve with a cinnamon stick and slice of lemon.

Sidewalk Sonata

This recipe comes by way of the bar team at Jefry's. Noix de la St Jean is a French walnut liqueur.

Add the egg white to a shaker without ice and shake vigorously for several seconds.

Add the remaining ingredients to the shaker with ice and shake again.

Pour into a rocks or old-fashioned glass.

Garnish with a peanut in its shell.

PEANUT OIL-INFUSED BOURBON

Add several drops of peanut oil to bourbon. Let stand for a couple of days at room temperature. Put the mixture in the freezer and remove the oil, which will harden and float to the top.

1 EGG WHITE

1¾ OZ. PEANUT OIL-INFUSED BOURBON (SEE RECIPE AT LEFT)

¾ OZ. TONKA SYRUP

⅓ OZ. NOIX DE LA ST JEAN

¾ OZ. FRESH LEMON JUICE

PEANUT IN SHELL (GARNISH)

Riverbank Reflections

1½ OZ. GIN

1 OZ. ORANGE BLOSSOM WATER

¾ OZ. CLARIFIED LIME JUICE

½ OZ. LILLET BLANC

½ OZ. SIMPLE SYRUP

LIME ZEST (GARNISH)

SKEWERED LUXARDO CHERRY (GARNISH)

We recommend choosing a botanical gin to match the orange blossom water and the aromatized aperitif wine Lillet Blanc. From the trees lining the streets to the flowers found all over Paris, this cocktail embodies the experience of walking along the Seine.

Add all the ingredients to a mixing glass and stir.

Pour the cocktail into a chilled Nick & Nora glass.

Garnish with a lime zest and skewered Luxardo cherry.

Painter's Palette

Campari's tangy rhubarb and bright orange notes make it a surprisingly good match for juicy watermelon in this luscious summer fizz. The liqueur's bracing bitterness is on full display, tempered by the rich body of Coco Lopez and the bright acidity of Champagne and lime.

Combine the gin, Campari, watermelon juice, lime juice, and Coco Lopez in a cocktail shaker filled with ice. Shake hard for 15 seconds, then strain into a chilled Champagne glass or chilled rocks glass filled with ice.

Top carefully with the chilled Champagne.

Garnish with watermelon cubes.

1 OZ. GIN

1 OZ. CAMPARI

1 OZ. FRESH WATERMELON JUICE (SEE PAGE 23)

½ OZ. FRESH, STRAINED LIME JUICE

½ OZ. COCO LOPEZ CREAM OF COCONUT

CHILLED CHAMPAGNE, TO TOP (ABOUT 1 OZ.)

WATERMELON ICE CUBES (GARNISH)

Beloved Bouquinistes

1½ OZ. STOLI ELITE VODKA

½ OZ. LEMON JUICE

½ OZ. LIQUORE ALLORO (BAY LEAF LIQUEUR)

½ OZ. SIMPLE SYRUP (SEE PAGE 9)

½ OZ. YZAGUIRRE BLANCO VERMOUTH

PINCH ERBA DEL VESCOVO

ROMAN MINT (GARNISH)

Sweet, sour, and herbal, this cocktail has the perfect balance of flavors. It brings together ingredients from Italy, Spain, and Russia—like a good book that can transport you anywhere in space and time.

Add all the ingredients to a shaker with ice and shake vigorously.

Double-strain into a chilled Mancino Alto glass.

Garnish with Roman mint.

Antique Treasure

This incredibly sophisticated cocktail will evolve with each sip—you'll experience sweetness and spiciness from the glass rim and dual rums, a hint of bittersweet from the Doppio Carvi, and some citrusy tang from the lime. Just like a beloved antique, this drink gives you an appreciation for the past while embracing the present.

Rim a Mancino Alto glass with green tea sugar and cardamom.

Add all the ingredients to a shaker with ice and shake vigorously.

Double-strain the cocktail into the Mancino Alto glass.

GREEN TEA SUGAR,
AS NEEDED, FOR THE RIM

GROUND CARDAMOM,
AS NEEDED, FOR THE RIM

1⅓ OZ. BLANC BLANC RUM

⅔ OZ. DOPPIO CARVI LIQUEUR

½ OZ. APPLETON ESTATE
SIGNATURE BLEND RUM

½ OZ. LIME JUICE

⅓ OZ. SIMPLE SYRUP

1 BARSPOON TAMARIND SYRUP

SMALL PINCH TURMERIC

PINCH CASSIA BARK

PINCH SZECHUAN PEPPERCORNS

1 OZ. GREY GOOSE VODKA

1 OZ. NOILLY PRAT DRY VERMOUTH

⅓ OZ. RABARBARO ZUCCA

ORANGE TWIST (GARNISH)

ANGEL HAIR CHILI (GARNISH)

The ingredients in this drink stretch artistic and geographic boundaries. Cassia (cinnamon), Szechuan pepper, French vermouth, and Russian vodka, scintillate and entice with every sip.

Grind the Szechuan pepper and cassia using a mortar and pestle.

Add the cassia, pepper, and remaining ingredients to a mixing glass with ice and stir gently.

Double-strain the cocktail into a coupette.

Garnish with an orange twist wrapped around a pinch of angel hair chili.

Water Under the Bridge

1½ OZ. VODKA

½ OZ. FRESH LIME JUICE

LIME WHEEL (GARNISH)

Like the serene waters of the Seine, this soothing sipper makes everything feel better. Whatever your troubles, cast them aside and enjoy this lovely cocktail.

Place the vodka and fresh lime juice in a mixing glass filled with ice and strain into a cocktail glass.

Garnish with a lime wheel.

OLGA
KORNELIA

LANGUAGE OF LOVE

Here, the everyday poetry of the French language takes center stage. Each cocktail is named after a familiar word or phrase, now reimagined in liquid form. These everyday expressions don't just sound charming—they're delicious!

Bonjour

2 OZ. COMMON MAN WHITE MOUNTAIN GINGER VODKA

8 LARGE MINT LEAVES

6 WILD STRAWBERRIES, OR 3 LARGE STORE-BOUGHT STRAWBERRIES, HALVED LENGTHWISE

1 SUGAR CUBE

MINT SPRIG (GARNISH)

STRAWBERRY SLICE (GARNISH)

Gently muddle the vodka, mint, berries, and sugar in the bottom of a rocks glass.

Fill the glass with ice, and stir until the sugar has completely dissolved.

Top off with more ice if necessary.

Garnish with a mint sprig and strawberry slice.

There's no more refreshing way to say hello than this semisweet, minty sipper with a kick of ginger (if using our suggested vodka choice).

Je T'aime

1 OZ. CITADELLE GIN

1 OZ. GRAPEFRUIT JUICE

1 OZ. ST-GERMAIN ELDERFLOWER LIQUEUR

¼ OZ. LIME JUICE

3 DASHES PEYCHAUD'S BITTERS

EDIBLE FLOWER (GARNISH)

This tart, floral, easy-drinking cocktail is as satisfying as the truest love, and as versatile as a long life lived together. You can change the gin for tequila, rum, or vodka, and it will always taste delicious.

Combine all the ingredients in a shaker filled with ice and shake vigorously.

Strain the cocktail into a coupe.

Garnish with a fresh edible flower.

Ooh La La

ROSE AND/OR VIOLETTE PETALS (GARNISH)

2 OZ. SNOW QUEEN VODKA, FROZEN

⅔ OZ. MARTINI BIANCO VERMOUTH

⅓ OZ. CHAMOMILE LIQUEUR

⅙ OZ. VIOLETTE LIQUEUR

LEMON ZEST (GARNISH)

This is a really stunning take on a traditional Martini, with the addition of violette liqueur to give it a floral aroma and a purple color, but also chamomile liqueur to add citrus notes to the drink. Martini purists might be skeptical, but give it a try—you might just be persuaded.

Dip the rim of the glass in something sticky, like simple syrup or honey, and affix rose and/or violette petals around the rim of the glass.

Pour all the ingredients into a mixing glass with ice and gently stir.

Strain the cocktail into a chilled martini glass.

Garnish with lemon zest.

½ OZ. BÉNÉDICTINE LIQUEUR

½ OZ. RYE WHISKEY

½ OZ. COGNAC

½ OZ. SWEET VERMOUTH

1 DASH PEYCHAUD'S BITTERS

1 DASH ANGOSTURA BITTERS

LEMON TWIST (GARNISH)

This sultry sipper defies all categorization. When you're not sure what to reach for, this cocktail is exactly the mystical and mysterious kind of drink that can meet any moment.

In a chilled old-fashioned glass with ice, combine all the ingredients. Stir.

Garnish with a lemon twist.

Bon Appetite

1½ OZ. GIN

¾ OZ. RASPBERRY SYRUP

¾ OZ. LIME JUICE

SPARKLING WATER OR SODA WATER, TO TOP

RASPBERRIES (GARNISH)

LIME (GARNISH)

MINT (GARNISH)

Add the gin, raspberry syrup, and lime juice to a Boston shaker.

Add ice and shake for 10 seconds.

Strain over fresh ice into a highball glass.

Top with sparkling water or soda water.

Garnish with raspberries, lime, and mint.

This delicious cocktail is light, herbal, and refreshing. If you want to make a nonalcoholic version, just leave out the gin.

This minty, creamy after-dinner cocktail, more commonly known as the Grasshopper, has been a dessert-like favorite of drinkers with a sweet tooth for almost a century.

1 OZ. GREEN CRÈME DE MENTHE

1 OZ. WHITE CRÈME DE CACAO

1 OZ. CREAM

In a cocktail tin filled with ice, combine all the ingredients. Shake.

Strain into a chilled cocktail glass.

1½ OZ. VODKA

¾ OZ. GRENADINE

½ OZ. LIMONCELLO

½ OZ. FRESH LEMON JUICE

CHAMPAGNE, TO TOP

LEMON WING (GARNISH)

This gorgeous, elegant drink isn't afraid to pack a punch. When you feel like celebrating, make a batch of these beauties and toast to the good life!

Add all the ingredients, except the Champagne, to a mixing glass and stir.

Pour the mixture into a Champagne flute, then top with Champagne.

Garnish with a lemon wing.

1½ OZ. GREEN MINT TEA

3–4 SPRIGS FRESH MINT

1 OZ. BOURBON, PREFERABLY BULLEIT

½ OZ. SIMPLE SYRUP (SEE PAGE 9)

FLOAT OF GINGER BEER (GARNISH)

LEMON WEDGE (GARNISH)

This minty, bubbly, boozy concoction is sure to make you feel awake and alive.

In a cocktail tin, shake all the ingredients and pour into a Collins glass half-filled with ice. Do not strain.

Top with ginger beer and garnish with a lemon wedge.

Honey transforms a basic Daiquiri into a Honeysuckle, and Champagne transforms a Honeysuckle into a crisp, complex fizz. The richness and body of the honey bolsters the clean, nuanced flavors of the white rum so that they both shine—a true partnership.

Combine the rum, honey syrup, and lime juice in a cocktail shaker filled with ice. Shake hard for 15 seconds, then strain into a chilled Champagne glass.

Top carefully with the chilled Champagne.

Garnish with a lime wheel and an edible flower.

2 OZ. WHITE RUM
(SUCH AS FLOR DE CAÑA)

¾ OZ. HONEY SYRUP
(SEE PAGE 30)

½ OZ. FRESH, STRAINED
LIME JUICE

CHILLED CHAMPAGNE, TO TOP
(ABOUT 1 OZ.)

LIME WHEEL (GARNISH)

EDIBLE FLOWER (GARNISH)

theView
FTOP TERRACE

Enchanté

2 OZ. BARR HILL GIN

½ OZ. FRESH LEMON JUICE

½ OZ. BUTTERFLY PEA FLOWER SIMPLE SYRUP

SODA WATER, TO TOP

PINK ORCHID (GARNISH)

LEMON WHEEL (GARNISH)

Add all the ingredients to a shaker filled with ice and shake vigorously.

Pour the cocktail into a Collins glass with ice.

Top with soda water and stir.

Garnish with a pink orchid and lemon wheel.

This gorgeous, vibrant cocktail is sure to elevate any experience. Day or night, this drink will add some sparkle to every occasion.

1⅓ OZ. VODKA VKA

⅔ OZ. ELDERFLOWER LIQUEUR

½ OZ. IL BORRO HONEY SYRUP, FLAVORED WITH ROSEMARY

½ OZ. LEMON JUICE

⅓ OZ. EGG WHITE

3 DROPS SALINE SOLUTION (SEE RECIPE AT RIGHT)

GRATED TUSCAN BLACK PEPPER (GARNISH)

ROSEMARY SPRIG (GARNISH)

Pour the vodka, elderflower liqueur, honey syrup, lemon juice, and egg white into a shaker without ice and dry-shake for 10 seconds.

Add the saline drops and ice to the shaker and shake more vigorously.

Pour all the contents of the shaker into a white wine glass without straining.

Garnish with grated black pepper and a rosemary sprig.

This smooth and delicate cocktail is ideal for a sunset sip. There are notes of citrus from the lemon juice, while the elderflower liqueur gives the drink more fragrance and a spicy sensation. The saline water adds a hint of salt, and the egg whites help froth up the drink.

SALINE SOLUTION

A mix of salt and water, saline solution can be used to enhance or balance flavors. To make it, use ¼ cup of salt and 1 cup of water, mix in a saucepan over heat until fully dissolved. Allow to cool and pour into a dropper bottle.

À la Mode

Ice cream may not be the first cocktail ingredient that comes to mind when you're thinking about your drinks, but it's a perfectly delightful topping if you're willing to be a little whimsical and adventurous.

1 OZ. SPICED RUM

2 OZ. COLA

1 SCOOP VANILLA ICE CREAM

Pour the spiced rum and cola into a pint glass.

Add a scoop of vanilla ice cream, and serve with a long spoon.

Femme Fatale

1 OZ. RITTENHOUSE 100 RYE (OR YOUR PREFERRED OVER-PROOF RYE)

2 TEASPOONS SIMPLE SYRUP (SEE PAGE 9)

CHAMPAGNE, TO TOP

LEMON PEEL (GARNISH)

This cocktail was created by cocktail expert Forest Collins of 52Martinis at the request of Cara Black to celebrate the 20th anniversary of her Aimée Leduc 90s-era detective series. Her fierce female lead solves murder mysteries in each Paris arrondissement and also has a penchant for leather stiletto boots and Champagne. (But we won't tell if you decide to sub in sparkling wine instead!)

Pour the rye and simple syrup into a chilled Champagne flute.

Express a lemon peel over the glass so the oils spray inside.

Top with Champagne.

Au Contraire

1½ OZ. SILVER TEQUILA

1½ OZ. FRESH GRAPEFRUIT JUICE

¾ OZ. JALAPEÑO-INFUSED VERMONT MAPLE SYRUP

½ OZ. MEZCAL

½ OZ. FRESH LIME JUICE

GRAPEFRUIT SLICE (GARNISH)

JALAPEÑO SLICE (GARNISH)

This concoction is full of daring contradictions. Take a chance and see if you can manage this thrilling blend of spicy jalapeño, smoky mezcal, and citrus juices.

Add all the ingredients to a cocktail shaker with ice and shake.

Strain the cocktail into a rocks glass over fresh ice.

Garnish with a slice of grapefruit and a slice of jalapeño.

C'est la Vie

2 OZ. TEQUILA REPOSADO INFUSED WITH COFFEE (SEE INSTRUCTIONS)

1 BARSPOON AGAVE SYRUP

3 DASHES ANGOSTURA BITTERS

CINNAMON STICK (GARNISH)

First, infuse the tequila reposado with coffee. Put 3 barspoons of coffee grounds in a filter submerged in 6 oz. of the tequila and let sit 4 hours to soak in the flavor.

Light a stick of cinnamon until it smolders on one end. Place on a plate and cover it with a rocks glass so the smoke accumulates in the glass.

Combine the infused tequila, agave syrup, and bitters in a mixing glass.

Upend the rock glass and strain the drink into it, adding a few cubes of ice.

This delicious drink was created by Candace Knyf as Death by Burrito's special during Paris's first-ever cocktail week in January 2015.

Bonsoir

1⅔ OZ. WOODFORD RESERVE BOURBON

⅔ OZ. BANANA LIQUEUR

⅙ OZ. KAHLÚA

⅙ OZ. DEMERARA SYRUP

2 DASHES ORANGE BITTERS

BANANA CH!P (GARNISH)

This sweet and fruity drink takes you right to the riverbank, as it not only tastes like a refreshing summer cocktail, but its color also resembles the perfect sunsets off the Seine.

Pour all the ingredients into a mixing glass with ice and stir.

Fill a rocks glass with a giant ice cube.

Strain the cocktail into the rocks glass.

Garnish with a banana chip.

MONUMENTAL MARVELS

Explore a lineup of cocktails named for the iconic sites and structures of Paris. Each concoction is a clear nod to the places that define this city's character. With recipes created in honor of landmarks like the Arc de Triomphe and La Tour Eiffel, drinking has never been quite so transportive.

Sacré-Cœur at Sunset

This strange little sipper has the complexity of the gorgeous architecture of Sacré-Cœur Basilica, with all the brilliance of a stunning sunset. These ingredients may seem like odd bedfellows. But, taken together, the aromatics on display sing like a chorus.

Fill a chilled rocks glass with crushed ice, then top with the tequila, lime juice, and cinnamon syrup. Stir lightly just until combined.

Top first with the chilled tonic water, then with the chilled lambrusco. Serve with a straw.

Garnish with a lime wheel and blackberry.

1½ OZ. TEQUILA

½ OZ. FRESH, STRAINED LIME JUICE

½ OZ. CINNAMON SYRUP (SEE PAGE 69)

2 OZ. CHILLED TONIC WATER

CHILLED LAMBRUSCO SECCO (DRY), TO TOP (1 OZ.)

LIME WHEEL (GARNISH)

BLACKBERRY (GARNISH)

SALT, FOR THE RIM

1½ OZ. SILVER TEQUILA

1½ OZ. ST-GERMAIN ELDERFLOWER LIQUEUR

1⅓ OZ. FRESH LIME JUICE

1 SPLASH SELTZER WATER, TO TOP (OPTIONAL)

EDIBLE FLOWERS (GARNISH)

LIME WHEEL (GARNISH)

MINT SPRIG (GARNISH)

Lost in the Louvre

This cocktail celebrates the most visited museum in the world. Like the Louvre, this drink is sure to dazzle and delight all who behold it.

Wet the rim of a wineglass and dip it into salt.

Place the tequila, St-Germain, and lime juice in a cocktail shaker, add ice, and shake until chilled.

Fill the glass with ice, strain the cocktail into the glass, top with the seltzer (if desired), and garnish with the edible flowers, lime wheel, and mint sprig.

2 OZ. TAMARIND-INFUSED VERMOUTH (SEE RECIPE AT RIGHT)

¾ OZ. ESPOLÒN BLANCO TEQUILA

⅙ OZ. MEZCAL NUESTRA SOLEDAD

2 DROPS MANDARIN BITTERS

EDIBLE FLOWERS (GARNISH)

The key to this drink is infusing the tangy sweetness of tamarind into vermouth, which takes a few days. But once you have the bottle ready, you can impress your guests. This exquisite cocktail combines the smoothness of tequila and smokiness of mezcal. It's a showstopper, much like that most beloved of Paris landmarks.

Add all the ingredients to a mixing glass with ice.

Strain into a coupette with two ice cubes.

Garnish with edible flowers.

TAMARIND-INFUSED VERMOUTH

Combine ½ cup tamarind paste and one bottle of Martini & Rossi Vermouth in a large jar. Seal the jar and shake well, then store it in a cool, dark place for 3 to 4 days. Strain the vermouth through a cheesecloth into a clean bottle and store the bottle in the refrigerator.

2 OZ. RYE WHISKEY

½ OZ. LEMON

½ OZ. MAPLE SYRUP

¼ OZ. SUZE

ABSINTHE, FOR MISTING

FRESH THYME (GARNISH)

Milling About Montmarte

This drink has all the layers and flavors of one of the most iconic districts in Paris. Montmartre's artistic history, bohemian atmosphere, and iconic landmarks are all celebrated in this delicious cocktail.

In a cocktail tin, combine all the ingredients with ice. Shake.

Strain into a coupe that has been misted with absinthe (see recipe below).

Garnish with a sprig of fresh thyme.

ABSINTHE MIST

Fill a small, travel-sized spray bottle with absinthe. Coat the inside of the glass with 1–2 sprays.

1 OZ. VODKA GUILLOTINE

⅔ OZ. ST-GERMAIN

½ OZ. SODA WATER

2¾ OZ. TAITTINGER CHAMPAGNE

1 OZ. CITRUS SHRUB

This cocktail was created by the talented team at the Bar Josephine in the iconic Hotel Lutetia. Drinking it, you'll feel as if you're traipsing down one of the most iconic streets in the world, surrounded by beauty and luxury.

Pour all the ingredients in a Collins glass over ice and stir.

Plans-Guides Blay, 26 rue Feydeau
75002 PARIS
E
S
93 SEINE ST. DENIS
ST-DENIS
LA COURNEUVE
DRANCY
AUBERVILLIERS
BOBIGNY
NOISY-LE-SEC
ROMAINVILLE
MONTREUIL
19
Buttes Chaumont
HAUTS DE SEI
PT. DE LEVALLOIS
BÉCON
Quai
N 308
Boulevard
Victor
Hugo
Rue Delaizement
PTE. MAILLOT
VICTOR-HUGO
R. DE
LA POMPE
INFÉRIEUR
Suresnes
Lac
St. Cloud

PEACH PUREE

Place four white peaches (washed, pitted, peeled, and sliced) into a large stainless steel bowl with 13½ ounces pinot grigio and two raspberries. After 3 days, remove the peaches and place them in an earthenware bowl and refrigerate for a few hours. Then place the peaches, the juice of one lemon, 60 grams sugar, and the pinot grigio in a blender and blend until the puree is completely smooth.

Visions Versailles

⅔ OZ. PEACH PUREE (SEE RECIPE AT LEFT)

3⅓ OZ. PROSECCO

SLICE OF PEACH (GARNISH)

This is truly the cocktail of royalty, from its refined taste to its gorgeous appearance. Princess Diana once confessed that this particular bellini was her favorite. It takes a few days to make the puree, but once it's done, this magical elixir will be a fan favorite amongst your friends.

Pour the peach puree and prosecco into a mixing glass filled with ice and quickly stir.

Strain the cocktail directly into a Champagne flute.

Garnish with a slice of peach.

J'adore les Jardins

1 SPRIG ROSEMARY

¾ OZ. GREEN CHARTREUSE

CHILLED CHAMPAGNE, TO TOP (ABOUT 3 OZ.)

¼ OZ. FRESH, STRAINED LIME JUICE

Much like the iconic gardens of Paris, there is something to be appreciated here no matter the season. In the winter months the alpine flavors of the liqueur really shine, but its intense herbal punch is utterly refreshing in the heat of summer, too.

Rub the sprig of rosemary around the inside of a chilled rocks glass, then set aside.

Pour the Chartreuse, chilled Champagne, and lime juice carefully into the glass, in that order. Gently slide in ice and place the rosemary sprig on top.

Opera Garnier

6 DASHES ANGOSTURA BITTERS

½ TO 1 TEASPOON SUGAR (TO TASTE)

2 OZ. FRENCH WHISKY

ORANGE TWIST (GARNISH)

Combine the bitters and sugar in the bottom of a rocks glass and muddle together to help the sugar dissolve.

Add the whisky and a large ice cube and stir.

Garnish with an orange zest.

This is a French take on the Old Fashioned, introducing Parisian flair to a classic cocktail.

2 OZ. STRAWBERRY PUREE

½ OZ. MANZANA VERDE

1 TABLESPOON FRESH LIME JUICE

BRUT CHAMPAGNE, TO TOP

STRAWBERRY (GARNISH)

This signature drink at the rooftop bar at the Raphael Hotel is fresh and breezy.

Shake the strawberry puree, Manzana Verde, and lime juice together together in a cocktail shaker with ice, and strain.

Serve in a chilled Champagne glass, topping off with Brut Champagne.

Garnish with a strawberry.

¾ OZ. LUXARDO BITTER BIANCO

¾ OZ. DOLIN BLANC VERMOUTH

½ OZ. DANTE LIMONCELLO

2 DASHES LEMON BITTERS

2½ OZ. PROSECCO

½ OZ. SAN PELLEGRINO

LEMON FLOWER (GARNISH)

Château Charm

This citrusy sipper transports you to the comfort and charm of the most beautiful homes in France. The bitter orange Bianco and Dolin Blanc dry vermouth are an unexpected but ideal pair to the bubbly vivaciousness of prosecco and San Pellegrino.

Fill a highball with one rectangular ice chunk.

Fill a shaker with ice and add the Luxardo, Dolin Blanc, limoncello, and lemon bitters and shake vigorously for 10 to 15 seconds.

Strain the mixture into the highball glass.

Top the drink with prosecco and San Pellegrino and gently stir.

Garnish with a lemon flower.

Stained Glass Sunbeams

This simple-to-make cocktail is sweet and fruity with just a hint of bitterness. It's a nice aperitif not only to sip but to admire, just as you would the gorgeous stained glass windows found in cathedrals across Paris.

Rim a Nick & Nora glass with sugar.

Add the grapes and pear pieces to the glass.

Add the brandy and vermouth to a mixing glass with ice and stir.

Strain the mixture into the glass.

Float an orange wheel on the surface of the liquid.

SUGAR, FOR THE GLASS RIM

¾ OZ. ITALIAN BRANDY

1¼ OZ. COCCHI STORICO

4 GRAPES (REFRIGERATED, GARNISH)

2 PEAR WEDGES (REFRIGERATED, GARNISH)

ORANGE WHEEL (REFRIGERATED, GARNISH)

½ LIME, CUT INTO SMALL PIECES

2 TEASPOONS BROWN SUGAR

2 OZ. CACHAÇA

DASH ORANGE BITTERS

SAFFRON POWDER, TO TOP

LIME WEDGE (GARNISH)

This slightly bitter but deliciously floral drink radiates with a bright yellow glow because of the saffron. Like the architectural wonder of Notre-Dame, this cocktail is a luminous marvel.

Add the lime and sugar to a medium tumbler and muddle together until the sugar is dissolved.

Add crushed ice to the glass to about two-thirds full.

Pour the cachaça and a dash of orange bitters over the ice.

Gently stir to combine the ingredients.

Top with a sprinkle of saffron powder.

Garnish with a lime wedge.

This colorful, eye-catching drink embodies the artistic spirit of one of the most important museums in France. With the largest collection of Impressionist and post-Impressionist masterpieces in the world, the Musée D'Orsay is a masterpiece in itself—and this drink captures that same creative flair.

In a cocktail tin, combine all the ingredients and shake vigorously for about 10 seconds.

Strain into a footed pilsner glass filled with pebble ice.

Drizzle 3 dashes of Peychaud's over top of the drink, and slip a lime wheel on the side.

1 OZ. BITTERMENS BÄSKA SNAPS

½ OZ. RUM, PREFERABLY BANKS 7

1½ OZ. PINEAPPLE JUICE

½ OZ. LIME JUICE

½ OZ. ORGEAT

PEYCHAUD'S BITTERS (GARNISH)

LIME WHEEL (GARNISH)

Gothic Grandeur

1⅓ OZ. PATRÓN SILVER

1 OZ. BUTTERFLY PEA FLOWER TEA

½ OZ. MARTINI AMBRATO

½ OZ. LEMON JUICE

⅓ OZ. OLEO CLEMENTINE SACCHARUM

This steely blue cocktail is simple to make but complex when it comes to flavor. The butterfly tea plays an important role in adding floral essence with every sip. The Patrón is key because it's incredibly smooth, while the Martini Ambrato gives the drink its sweetness. This drink is a feast for the eyes, nose, and taste buds that works in perfect harmony.

Add all the ingredients to a shaker with ice. Shake vigorously for 10 seconds.

Strain the cocktail into a highball glass over a large cube of ice.

METRIC CONVERSIONS

US Measurement	Approximate Metric Liquid Measurement	Approximate Metric Dry Measurement
1 teaspoon	5 ml	5 g
1 tablespoon or ½ ounce	15 ml	14 g
1 ounce or ⅛ cup	30 ml	29 g
¼ cup or 2 ounces	60 ml	57 g
⅓ cup	80 ml	76 g
½ cup or 4 ounces	120 ml	113 g
⅔ cup	160 ml	151 g
¾ cup or 6 ounces	180 ml	170 g
1 cup or 8 ounces or ½ pint	240 ml	227 g
1½ cups or 12 ounces	350 ml	340 g
2 cups or 1 pint or 16 ounces	475 ml	454 g
3 cups or 1½ pints	700 ml	680 g
4 cups or 2 pints or 1 quart	950 ml	908 g

CADEAU DÉCO LINGE DE MAISON

INDEX

About CIDER MILL PRESS BOOK PUBLISHERS

Cider Mill Press publishes exceptional books that combine creativity and craftsmanship. As an imprint of HarperCollins Focus, we specialize in premium cookbooks, cocktail and spirits guides, and illustrated gift books, all distinguished by compelling content, striking design, and a commitment to quality in every detail. Cider Mill Press sets the standard for books that inform, inspire, and elevate everyday moments. Learn more at cidermillpress.com.

"Where Good Books Are Ready for Press"
501 Nelson Place
Nashville, Tennessee 37214 USA